Operation Awesome: Cracking the Code with Math

Rekha Kumari

Published by rekharaj, 2024.

OPERATION AWESOME: CRACKING THE CODE WITH MATH

First edition. April 18, 2024.

ISBN: 979-8224877485

Written by Rekha Kumari.

Table of Contents

Dedication

To the eager minds of young mathematicians everywhere,

This book is dedicated to you. Within these pages lie the keys to unlocking the mysteries of mathematics, and I hope it ignites a spark within you—a passion for numbers, patterns, and problem-solving.

May you embark on a journey of exploration and discovery, fueled by curiosity and guided by the principles shared here?

Let this book be your companion as you navigate the fascinating world of math, equipping you with the tools and knowledge to become true masters of the subject.

Here's to endless curiosity, boundless imagination, and the thrilling adventure of learning.

With warm regards,

Rekha Kumari

The Lady Entrepreneur & Educator

Legal Disclaimer

Copyright@Rekha Kumari - 2024

The publisher and the author disclaim any liability for any damages or losses arising directly or indirectly from the use of this book.

All information contained herein is offered for entertainment and educational purposes only and does not constitute professional advice or instruction.

Names, characters, places, and incidents are either products of the author's imagination or used fictitiously.

Any resemblance to real persons, living or deceased, or to actual events is purely coincidental.

Publication of any part or any moral or lesson for commercial uses is strictly prohibited.

Artificial Intelligence Disclaimer

Copyright@Rekha Kumari - 2024

While the story and illustrations within this book were created with the assistance of artificial intelligence, the core concept, plot development, and overall message originated with a human author.

The purpose of this AI integration is to explore the potential of artificial intelligence in creating engaging and educational content for children.

This disclaimer clarifies that AI was used as a tool in the creative process, but the core ideas and themes are from a human author.

It also emphasizes the book's focus on educating children about the potential of AI.

Preface

Hey there, awesome reader!

Ever wished you could be a detective with a knack for numbers?

Well, dust off your magnifying glass and sharpen your pencils, because you're about to embark on a thrilling adventure where **YOU** are the star!

This isn't your typical math book (yawn!). **"Operation Awesome: Cracking the Code with Math"** is packed with **mind-bending puzzles, secret codes, and a mystery so puzzling, only a math whiz like you can crack it!**

Here's what makes this book extra special:

- **Become a Math Mastermind:** We'll tackle cool math concepts like addition, subtraction, percentages, and more, all while unraveling a sneaky mystery. Learning has never been so much fun!

- **Unlock the Clues:** Prepare to decipher cryptic messages, solve brain-busting puzzles, and use your math skills to follow a trail of clues. Get ready to put your detective skills to the test!

- **Boost Your Confidence:** As you progress through the story, you'll discover the power of math in solving real-world problems. Math isn't just about numbers anymore, it's your secret weapon for success!

So, are you ready to join Maya and Ben on their thrilling math adventure?

Buckle up, grab your thinking cap, and get ready to **crack the code and become an Operation Awesome! Math Detective!**

Rekha Kumari

The Lady Entrepreneur & Educator

Open Talk with Rekha Kumari

Hey there, young mathematicians!

As an author who loves both stories and numbers, I've always dreamed of creating a book that would make learning math **as exciting as cracking a secret code!**

"Operation Awesome: Cracking the Code with Math" is finally here, and I believe it represents a real milestone in how kids can build their math expertise.

Here's why this book is different:

- **Learning by Doing:** Forget boring drills and worksheets! This book throws you right into a thrilling mystery where you use math skills to solve puzzles and follow clues. It's learning by doing, and trust me, it's way more fun than memorizing formulas!

- **Building Confidence:** As you crack codes and solve challenges, you'll see how powerful math can be. You'll learn to think critically, solve problems creatively, and gain the confidence to tackle any math problem that comes your way.

- **A Love of Math, Not a Fear:** Let's face it, some kids struggle with math. This book aims to change that! By wrapping math concepts in a fun, engaging story, we hope to spark a love of learning that will stay with you throughout your academic journey.

"Operation Awesome: Cracking the Code with Math" isn't just a book, it's an **adventure in math mastery**. It's a chance to unlock your potential and discover the incredible world of numbers. So, are you ready to become an awesome math detective?

Let's get cracking!

Rekha Kumari

The Lady Entrepreneur & Educator

Chapter 1: The Case of the Missing Cookies

◈ **Plot:** Maya wakes up to find her freshly baked cookies missing. A mysterious note with a coded message is left behind.

◈ **Defining Number:** Whole Numbers (Counting Numbers)

◈ **Activities:** Counting cookies, identifying missing numbers in a sequence.

◈ **Tips & Tricks:** Skip counting by 1s to find the total number of cookies.

Mmm, the smell of freshly baked cookies!
Maya skipped into the kitchen, her stomach grumbling happily. But wait a minute... something was wrong!

The plate that was supposed to be overflowing with warm, gooey cookies was completely empty!

"Mom! Dad!" Maya called out, a worried frown spreading across her face. "Where are all the cookies?"

Just then, Maya spotted a small piece of paper tucked under a corner of the counter. It looked like a note, but instead of words, it had strange symbols on it.

"This is weird," Maya mumbled, picking up the note. It looked like a bunch of squiggles and circles, but it also had some numbers mixed in.

Could this have something to do with the missing cookies?

Maya's detective senses were tingling!

She grabbed a magnifying glass (because what good detective is complete without one?) and started examining the note.

One thing Maya knew for sure – those squiggles and circles wouldn't tell her anything on their own.

But maybe the numbers could help?

There were several numbers written out, like 1, 2, 3, and 4. Maya recognized these – they were the counting numbers!

Aha! Maybe these numbers were a clue!

But what did they mean?

Maya sat down at the kitchen table, the mysterious note spread out before her.

Here's where you come in, detective!

Can you help Maya figure out the code and find out what happened to her missing cookies?

Let's try this:

1. **Counting Cookies:** Imagine there were a dozen delicious cookies on the plate before they vanished. Let's start by counting all the numbers written on the note. How many numbers can you find?
2. **Missing in Action:** Now, look closely at the numbers. Are there any numbers missing in sequence? For example, if you see 1, 2, 4, there seems to be a missing number – 3!
3. **Skip Counting:** Counting by 1s can take a while. Can you skip count by 1s to see if the total number of written numbers matches the number of missing cookies?

If you manage to crack this clue, Maya might just be one step closer to uncovering the case of the missing cookies!

Remember, detective work involves patience, observation, and a little bit of math magic!

Let Us Learn About Numbers

A number is a mathematical symbol used to represent quantity. We use numbers for counting, measuring, and ordering things. There are different types of numbers, each with specific properties:

- **Natural Numbers (Counting Numbers):** These are the positive whole numbers used for counting, starting from 1 and going on infinitely. Examples: 1, 2, 3, 4, 5...
- **Whole Numbers:** These include natural numbers and zero (0). They represent whole objects and are not fractions or decimals. Examples: 0, 1, 2, 3, 4, 5...
- **Integers:** These include whole numbers, their negatives, and zero. Integers represent whole quantities, positive or negative. Examples: -5, -4, -3, 0, 1, 2, 3...
- **Rational Numbers:** These numbers can be expressed as a

fraction where the numerator and denominator are integers (denominator cannot be zero). They represent parts of a whole or ratios between quantities. Examples: 1/2, 3/4, -5/7, 1.5 (which can be written as 3/2).

- **Irrational Numbers:** These numbers cannot be expressed as a simple fraction. Their decimal representation never ends or repeats in a predictable pattern. Examples: Pi ($\pi \approx 3.14159$), the square root of 2 ($\sqrt{2} \approx 1.41421$).

- **Real Numbers:** These include rational and irrational numbers. They represent all numbers on the number line, both positive and negative.

- **Complex Numbers:** These numbers include real numbers and imaginary unit "i" (where $i = \sqrt{-1}$). They are expressed in the form a + bi, where a and b are real numbers. Examples: 3+2i, 5i, -1-7i.

These are some of the common types of numbers. Depending on the area of mathematics, there can be other specialized types of numbers as well.

Learn These Name of Numbers with Rhyme

Counting apples, one, two, three,
Those are whole numbers, you and me!
Zero's lonely, all alone,
But joins the fun to make them known.
Integers, next we'll meet the crew,
Positive, negative, all brand new!
Three steps forward, then two back,
Counting both ways on the number track.
Fractions come, a slice of pie,
One of eight, how big a bite?
Half a sandwich, neat and fair,

Sharing treats without a care.
Decimals too, with points so fine,
Three point one four, a number line.
Lengths and weights, so very small,
Numbers help us measure all.
Don't forget, there's more to find,
Irrational numbers, one of a kind!
Square root of two, a mystery,
Its decimal goes on endlessly.
So many numbers, big and small,
Helping us count and measure all!
From tiny ants to galaxies grand,
Numbers help us understand.

Chapter 2: The Puzzling Trail Mix

◇ **Plot:** Maya and her friend Ben decipher the first clue, leading them to the park where they find a bag of trail mix with coded weights on each ingredient.

◇ **Defining Number:** Addition

◇ **Activities:** Weighing out ingredients, solving addition problems to find the total weight of the trail mix.

◇ **Tips & Tricks:** Use pictures or manipulatives to represent addition problems.

Armed with her detective skills and a keen eye for numbers, **Maya knew she couldn't crack this case alone!**

So, she called her best friend, Ben, who was just as excited about mysteries as she was.

Together, they studied the strange symbols on the note. After some head-scratching and a few giggles at the silly squiggles, they noticed a pattern. One of the symbols seemed to appear next to each number!

"Maybe these symbols represent the missing cookies!" Ben exclaimed.

Eureka! Maya's eyes lit up. "That makes sense!

But what about the other symbols?

Do you think they have something to do with where the cookies went?"

Suddenly, they noticed a small arrow pointing downwards at the bottom of the note. Below it, there were more symbols, but this time, they were paired with numbers in a different way.

"These numbers look different," Ben observed. "They seem to be getting bigger and bigger."

Intrigued, Maya took another look. "You're right!

It's like they're adding things up!"

A light bulb went off in Maya's head!

Could these be the weights of something?

Maybe the culprit used the first clue to tell them how many cookies were missing, and now they were giving a clue about where to find them!

The answer might be hiding in plain sight!

Maya grabbed her backpack and looked at Ben with a determined grin. "Let's go check the park!

Remember, that arrow pointed downwards, so maybe the answer is somewhere lower than our house."

The park was their next stop!

After searching every nook and cranny, they finally spotted it – a bright red backpack nestled under a shady tree. Inside the backpack, they found a bag of trail mix!

But this wasn't any ordinary trail mix. Each ingredient had a tiny sticker with a number on it!

Now, it was time for some real math detective work!
Here's your challenge, detectives!

- **Addition Mission:** Look at the stickers on the trail mix ingredients. Can you add up the numbers on each sticker? Do you think the sum (total) of these numbers matches the weights mentioned in the mysterious note?
- **Weighty Clue:** Maybe the culprit used the weights as a clue to where they hid the missing cookies! Do the numbers on the stickers seem to point to a specific location in the park?

By using your addition skills, you can help Maya and Ben crack this next puzzle!

Remember, addition is like putting things together. It helps us find the total amount when we combine things!

Learn Addition of Numbers with Rhyme

One red apple, round and bright,
Two yellow lemons, shining light.
Add them together, what do we find?
Three juicy fruits, a yummy kind!
Three bluebirds singing in a tree,
Five fluffy clouds for all to see.
Add them together, don't you fret,
Eight fluffy friends, we won't forget!
Four ladybugs with spots so red,
Six busy bees buzzing ahead.
Add them together, the answer's clear,

Ten little friends, without a fear!
So adding numbers, big or small,
Brings things together, one and all.
Counting them up, it's lots of fun,
Addition magic, everyone!

Chapter 3: The Secret Subway Code

◇ **Plot:** The weight clue points to a specific subway station. Decoded symbols on a map lead them to find a hidden message.

◇ **Defining Number:** Subtraction

◇ **Activities:** Creating subtraction problems based on subway fares, finding the difference between stations.

◇ **Tips & Tricks:** Relate subtraction to "taking away" from a whole number.

Their detective instincts tingling, Maya and Ben eagerly examined the weights on the trail mix ingredients. They added each number meticulously, their pencils flying across the paper.

"Hey, look!" Ben exclaimed, pointing at their calculations. "The sum of these weights matches one of the numbers on the note with the downwards arrow!"

Excitement bubbled in Maya's chest!

This must be the clue leading them to the missing cookies!

But where exactly?

They looked back at the mysterious note. Underneath the symbol paired with the weight they just matched, there were more symbols – this time, arranged around a small map of their town!

Aha! This map might be the key!

Maya grabbed a magnifying glass and started scrutinizing the symbols near their neighborhood. Suddenly, she noticed something strange. Some of the symbols on the map seemed to have lines drawn through them, like they were crossed out!

"Ben, look!" Maya called out, pointing at the crossed-out symbols. "Do you think these have something to do with the weights again?"

Ben tilted his head in thought. "Maybe!

Remember, the weights seemed to be getting bigger in the note. What if these crossed-out symbols represent numbers that need to be taken away from the weight we just calculated?"

A new challenge emerged!

Could this be subtraction in disguise?

Here's your math mission, detectives!

- **Subtraction Showdown:** Look at the weight you calculated from the trail mix and the crossed-out symbols on the map. Can you use subtraction to find the difference between the two?

- **Station Stop:** Maybe the difference you calculated points to a specific location! Can you find a subway station on the map whose number matches the result of your subtraction?

By using your subtraction skills, you can help Maya and Ben unlock the secret of the subway map!

Remember, subtraction is like taking away a part to find what remains. Use your detective skills and sharpen your pencils, because the next clue might be hiding in plain sight at a subway station!

Learn Subtraction of Numbers with Rhyme

Five cookies on a plate so high,
Two get eaten, with a happy sigh.
Five take away two, how many stay?
Three yummy cookies, left for play!
Seven ladybugs upon a leaf,
Three fly away, with happy grief.
Seven minus three, can you guess right?
Four ladybugs still taking flight!
Ten bouncy balls, so fun to see,
Four roll away, beneath the tree.
Ten take away four, what's left behind?
Six bouncy balls, of a happy kind!
Subtracting numbers, don't you fret,
It's like taking some things, and not all yet.
We find the difference, clear and true,
How many left, it's up to you!

Chapter 4: The Encrypted Library Card

◇ **Plot:** The hidden message mentions a library book with an encrypted code on the card.

◇ **Defining Number:** Multiplication

◇ **Activities:** Decoding multiplication problems hidden within the library card catalog system, finding the product of multiples.

◇ **Tips & Tricks:** Use multiplication tables or repeated addition to solve problems.

Following the trail of crossed-out symbols and subtraction, Maya and Ben found themselves standing in front of a bustling subway station. Relief washed over them – they were on the right track!

The hidden message on the map pointed to a specific subway line and a number that corresponded to a stop. As the train rattled along the tracks, Maya couldn't help but feel a thrill of excitement.

Were they finally getting closer to finding the missing cookies?

When they reached their stop, they hurried out of the station and followed a series of cryptic arrows scrawled on a nearby wall. These arrows led them to a familiar place – their local library!

"A library?"

Ben scratched his head, surprised. "What could missing cookies have to do with books?"

Just then, Maya spotted a worn-out book tucked away on a dusty shelf. Its title was strange – "The Adventures of Captain Cipher." But what truly caught their eye was the library card tucked inside the front cover.

"Look!" Maya exclaimed, pointing excitedly at the card. "There are numbers written here, but they're all jumbled up!"

Indeed, the library card was covered in a seemingly random string of numbers. But something about the way they were arranged sparked a memory in Maya's mind.

"Wait a minute!" she exclaimed, snapping her fingers. "Remember how the weights on the trail mix added up to a specific number?

Maybe these numbers need to be multiplied together!"

Multiplication?

Ben pondered this idea. "But why multiply?

Wouldn't adding them work?"

Maya shook her head. "Think about it, Ben. If the weights on the trail mix added up to the total weight, then why would the message lead us here?

Maybe multiplying these numbers gives us a clue about something inside the library!"

A new puzzle unfolded before them!

Could multiplication be the key to deciphering the library card code?

Here's your math challenge, detectives!

- **Multiplication Mission:** Take a closer look at the jumbled numbers on the library card. Can you use multiplication to find the product (result) of these numbers?
- **Library Location:** Maybe the product you calculated refers to a specific location within the library. Could it be a Dewey Decimal number (a library classification system) or a shelf number leading to another clue?

Sharpen your pencils, detectives, and put your multiplication skills to the test!

By solving this code, you might just help Maya and Ben unlock the secrets hidden within the library walls!

Learn Multiplication of Numbers with Rhyme

Three fluffy sheep in a green field graze,
Three times one sheep, in a counting daze.
Three fluffy sheep, that's what we see,
Multiplication makes three times one agree!
Four ladybugs land on a bright red rose,
Two times two, their tiny house it grows.
Four ladybugs, a buzzing sight,
Two times two makes counting just right!
Five hungry birds sing a morning tune,
Three seeds each, eaten very soon.
Five times three, a feast so grand,
Multiplication helps us understand!

Skip counting friends, in a happy row,
Four times four, how the numbers grow!
Sixteen friends, with a joyful shout,
Multiplication makes us figure it out!
So times them up, these numbers bold,
A shortcut to counting, stories untold.
Multiplying makes things fast and fun,
Answers galore, under the sun!

Chapter 5: The Divisibility Challenge

◇ **Plot:** The library book reveals a series of numbers with a clue about "divisibility."

◇ **Defining Number:** Division

◇ **Activities:** Identifying factors and multiples, solving division problems to find remainders.

◇ **Tips & Tricks:** Relate division to "sharing" a whole number into equal groups.

Following Maya's hunch, they grabbed a pen and paper and started multiplying the jumbled numbers on the library card. After a few scribbles and calculations, they arrived at a final answer – a large, impressive number!

"Wow, that's a big number!" Ben whistled. "But what does it mean?"

They flipped through the pages of "The Adventures of Captain Cipher," hoping to find a clue. Nestled amongst the fantastical tales of pirates and hidden treasures, they stumbled upon a section titled "The Mystery of Divisibility."

The passage spoke of a secret code where some numbers could be neatly divided (split equally) by others, revealing hidden messages. Intrigued, Maya scanned the library card again. This time, she noticed something interesting – some of the numbers used in the multiplication problem seemed to be written in a different color!

"Maybe these colored numbers are the key!" Maya exclaimed.

Ben's eyes widened. "Do you think we need to divide the big number we got by these colored numbers?"

Division?

A new challenge emerged!

Could this be the answer to Captain Cipher's divisibility code?

Calling all math detectives!

Here's your mission:

- **Division Dojo:** Look at the large number you obtained from multiplying the library card code. Now, take a closer look at the colored numbers. Can you divide the big number by each of the colored numbers separately?

- **Remainder Reveal:** When you divide a number, sometimes you get a remainder (a leftover amount). In this case, pay close attention to the remainders you get after each division. Do any of the remainders match specific page numbers in Captain Cipher's book?

By using your division skills, you can help Maya and Ben crack Captain Cipher's code!

Remember, division is like splitting something into equal groups and finding out how many groups you get, or how much is leftover after the splitting is done. Use your detective skills and sharpen your pencils, because the next clue might be hiding within the pages of a mysterious book!

Learn Division of Numbers with Rhyme

Six juicy cookies on a plate so high,
Sharing with two friends, way up in the sky.
Six divided by two, what will we find?
Three cookies each, a treat for every kind!
Eight colorful candies in a shiny jar,
Splitting them fairly, near and far.
Eight divided by two, don't you frown,
Four candies each, yum, gobble them down!
Twelve bouncing balls in a happy bunch,
Sharing with three friends, at lunchtime lunch.
Twelve divided by three, how many per hand?
Four bouncy balls, fun across the land!
Division's magic, like a sharing spree,
Splitting things up, one, two, three!
The bigger number, we cut in parts,
Giving each friend, equal happy hearts!

Chapter 6: The Mysterious Lock Cipher

◈ **Plot:** The kids find a locked box with a keypad that requires a specific code based on divisibility rules.

◈ **Defining Number:** Prime Numbers

◈ **Activities:** Identifying prime numbers using divisibility rules, creating a list of prime numbers within a range.

◈ **Tips & Tricks:** Use a sieve method to identify prime numbers systematically.

Following the trail of divisibility, Maya and Ben eagerly divided their large number by each of the colored numbers. The calculations flew across their notebooks, leaving behind a trail of remainders. Anticipation hung heavy in the air – would any of these remainders unlock the secrets hidden within Captain Cipher's book?

Suddenly, Ben slammed his pencil down on the table, his eyes gleaming with excitement. "Look Maya! One of the remainders matches a page number in the book!"

They quickly flipped to the designated page, their hearts pounding with anticipation. There, staring back at them, was a peculiar illustration – a locked box with a keypad and a series of cryptic symbols.

"This must be the final challenge!" Maya exclaimed, a determined glint in her eyes.

But how to unlock the box?

The illustration seemed to hold the key. It depicted various numbers arranged in a specific way, along with arrows pointing in different directions.

As they examined the illustration closer, a new concept dawned on Maya. "Ben," she said slowly, "what if these numbers are the code to unlock the box? But how do we choose which ones to use?"

Ben's brow furrowed in thought. Then, a light bulb seemed to flicker on above his head. "Maybe not all the numbers are important!

Remember Captain Cipher's talk about divisibility?

What if we only use the numbers that can't be divided evenly by any other number on the keypad?"

Prime Numbers!

This was a new twist in the case!

Could prime numbers be the key to unlocking the mysterious box?

Calling all math detectives!

Here's the challenge:

- **Prime Patrol:** Look at the illustration of the keypad on the page. Can you identify all the numbers that cannot be divided evenly by any other number on the keypad (except 1 and itself)? These special numbers are called prime numbers.
- **Codebreaker Countdown:** Once you've identified the prime numbers, use the illustration's arrows to determine the order in which you should enter them on the keypad. Can you crack the code and unlock the secrets hidden within the mysterious box?

By using your knowledge of prime numbers and following the clues in the illustration, you can help Maya and Ben unlock the final puzzle in Captain Cipher's adventure!

Remember, prime numbers are special whole numbers that can only be divided evenly by 1 and themselves. Use your detective skills and crack the code to see what awaits them inside the box!

Let Us Learn About Prime And Composite Numbers

Prime Numbers:

A prime number is a whole number greater than 1 that has exactly two distinct positive divisors: 1 and itself. In simpler terms, a prime number can only be divided evenly by 1 and itself without any remainder.

- Examples: 2, 3, 5, 7, 11, 13, 17, 19

Composite Numbers:

A composite number is a whole number greater than 1 that has more than two distinct positive divisors. Unlike primes, composite numbers can be divided evenly by at least one other number besides 1 and itself.

- Examples: 4 (divisible by 1, 2, and 4), 6 (divisible by 1, 2, 3, and 6), 8 (divisible by 1, 2, 4, and 8), 9 (divisible by 1, 3, and 9), 10 (divisible by 1, 2, 5, and 10)

10 Key Points about Prime and Composite Numbers:

1. **1 is not prime or composite:** It only has one divisor (itself), which doesn't satisfy the definition of a prime number.
2. **Even numbers greater than 2 are composite:** Every even number greater than 2 can be divided by 2, making it composite.
3. **Prime numbers are infinite:** There's no limit to the number of prime numbers, although finding them gets progressively difficult.
4. **Fundamental Theorem of Arithmetic:** Every positive integer can be expressed as a unique product of prime numbers (prime factorization).
5. **Primes play a crucial role in cryptography:** Their properties are used to create secure encryption methods that protect data.
6. **Primality testing:** There are algorithms to determine if a number is prime, but finding large primes efficiently remains an active area of research.
7. **Goldbach's conjecture:** Every even integer greater than 2 can be expressed as the sum of two prime numbers (not yet proven).
8. **Twin primes:** These are prime numbers that differ by 2, like (3, 5) or (11, 13). They are infinitely rare, but mathematicians haven't proven it.
9. **Mersenne primes:** These are prime numbers of the form $2^p - 1$, where p is also prime. They are used in generating random numbers.
10. **Prime hunting:** There are ongoing projects dedicated to finding the largest known prime numbers, pushing the

boundaries of computational power.

Learn Prime Numbers with Rhyme

Numbers aplenty, a counting crew,
But some are special, a select few.
These prime numbers stand out, you see,
Divisible only by one and themselves, that's the key!
Two is the first, a lonely prime,
Standing alone, across space and time.
Three comes next, a perfect pick,
Divisible only by one and quick!
Five joins the club, a high number friend,
Divisible by one, its journey won't end.
Seven's next, a lucky roll,
Divisible by one, making it whole.
Eleven appears, a friend so bright,
Divisible by one, shining ever so light.
Thirteen we meet, but it's not quite right,
Divisible by three, it loses the fight.
Primes are special, a mysterious bunch,
Their patterns we seek, with a thoughtful hunch.
They build up the world, in a hidden way,
From grains of sand to stars that play.
So next time you count, don't just zoom ahead,
Look for the primes, in your number bed.
These special friends, with their unique rhyme,
Are the building blocks, of space and time!

Chapter 7: Following the Treasure Map

◇ **Plot:** Inside the box, they find a treasure map with coded distances and directions.

◇ **Defining Number:** Fractions

◇ **Activities:** Identifying fractions on a map scale, solving problems to find distances based on fractional measurements.

◇ **Tips & Tricks:** Relate fractions to parts of a whole, use visuals to represent fractions.

Relief washed over Maya and Ben as the satisfying click of the unlocked box filled the air. Inside, nestled amongst soft packing peanuts, lay a rolled-up piece of parchment.

Unfurling it with trembling hands, they discovered a treasure map!

But this wasn't any ordinary map. Instead of familiar streets and landmarks, it was filled with strange symbols and lines marked with curious fractions like ½, ¼, and ¾.

"What are these weird fractions doing on a map?"

Ben scratched his head, a hint of confusion in his voice.

Maya, ever the optimist, grinned. "Maybe they're the key to finding the missing cookies!

Remember how we used numbers to solve all the other puzzles?

Maybe these fractions tell us how far we need to walk in different directions!"

Fractions?

This was a new twist in their treasure hunt!

Could understanding fractions be the key to deciphering the map?

Calling all math detectives!

Here's your mission:

- **Fraction Frenzy:** Take a closer look at the map symbols and the lines connecting them. Each line has a fraction written next to it. Can you interpret these fractions as distances? For example, ½ might mean you need to walk half the length of the line.

- **Treasure Trail:** Now that you understand the distances represented by the fractions, follow the map's instructions! Start from the marked starting point and use the fractions as your guide. In what direction should you walk first, and for how far (based on the fraction)?

By mastering fractions, you can help Maya and Ben follow the cryptic clues on the map and get one step closer to uncovering the location of the missing cookies – and maybe even the culprit behind this whole mystery!

Remember, fractions represent parts of a whole, and they can be used to measure distances on a map just like numbers!

Let Us Learn About Fraction And Its Types

A fraction represents a part of a whole or a collection of objects. It tells you how many pieces you have out of a total number of pieces. Fractions are written with two numbers separated by a horizontal line.

- The top number, called the **numerator**, indicates the number of parts you consider.
- The bottom number, called the **denominator**, represents the total number of equal parts the whole has been divided into.

Here are the different types of fractions:

1. Proper Fractions:

- The numerator is **smaller** than the denominator.
- The fraction represents a part that is **less than the whole**.
- Example: 1/2 (one out of two slices of pie)

2. Improper Fractions:

- The numerator is **larger** than the denominator, or they are equal.
- The fraction represents a part that is **equal to or greater than the whole**.
- Improper fractions can sometimes be converted to mixed numbers (see below).

- Example: 3/2 (more than two slices of pie - this could be cut into 1 whole pie and 1/2 slice leftover)

3. Mixed Numbers:

- A combination of a whole number and a proper fraction.
- It represents a whole and some additional parts of the whole.
- Example: 1 1/2 (1 whole pie and 1/2 slice leftover)

4. Equivalent Fractions:

- Fractions that represent the same quantity even though they are written differently.
- We can obtain equivalent fractions by multiplying or dividing the numerator and denominator by the same number (except for zero).
- Example: 1/2 is equivalent to 2/4 (both represent half of something)

Learn Fractions with Rhyme

A pizza round, so cheesy and grand,
Cut into eight, for a yummy band.
One slice you eat, with a happy sigh,
That's one out of eight, a fraction so high!
A chocolate cake, with layers so sweet,
Divided in half, a delicious treat.
Half for you, and half for your friend,
Sharing fractions, the fun will never end!
Three juicy oranges, hanging so bright,
You take a big slice, with all your might.
One-third of the orange, a healthy delight,
Fractions help us share things just right!
A pie cut in four, with berries so red,

Two slices you take, before going to bed.
Two out of four, your tummy is full,
Fractions help us measure, by the spoonful!
So fractions aren't scary, don't you fret,
They're pieces of a whole, we haven't met.
Sharing and measuring, big or small,
Fractions help us understand it all!

Chapter 8: The Tricky Time Trial

Decimals Dash!

◇ **Plot:** The map leads to a hidden location with a time trial challenge involving coded time intervals.

◇ **Defining Number:** Decimals

◇ **Activities:** Converting fractions to decimals, solving problems involving elapsed time with decimals.

◇ **Tips & Tricks:** Use a place value table to understand the position of decimals.

Following the map's cryptic instructions, Maya and Ben navigated a maze of winding streets and hidden alleyways. Each fraction on the map guided them with surprising accuracy, leading them closer and closer to their destination. Finally, they arrived at a seemingly ordinary park bench, marked with a small red X on the map.

"This is it?"

Ben asked, disappointment tinging his voice. "Just a park bench?"

Suddenly, a hidden compartment popped open beneath the seat, revealing a digital timer counting down from 60.00 seconds!

"Whoa!

A time trial!" Maya exclaimed, adrenaline coursing through her veins. "The map must have led us to a secret challenge!"

Beside the timer, a small screen displayed a series of cryptic messages. Each message contained a jumble of numbers with decimal points, like 3.2, 1.75, and 4.8.

"What do these numbers mean?" Ben furrowed his brow, a puzzled expression crossing his face.

"Maybe they're times!"

Maya gasped, a realization dawning on her.

"Remember how we learned about decimals in math class?

They can represent parts of a whole, just like fractions!"

Decimals?

This was a new hurdle in their race against time!

Could understanding decimals be the key to completing the challenge?

Calling all math detectives!

Here's your mission:

- **Decimal Decoder:** Look at the jumbled numbers displayed on the screen. Can you interpret them as times based on decimals? For example, 3.2 might represent 3 whole seconds and 2 tenths of a second.
- **Time Trial Triumph:** Now that you understand the times represented by the decimals, pay close attention to the order of the messages. These messages might be instructions that need to be completed within the specified time limits. Can you decipher the instructions and complete them all before the timer reaches zero?

By mastering decimals and thinking quickly, you can help Maya and Ben conquer the time trial challenge!

Remember, decimals are a way to represent parts of a whole, often used to measure time with greater precision than whole seconds. Crack the code, complete the tasks within the time limits, and see what awaits them on the other side!

Let Us Learn About Decimal Number And Its Types

A decimal number is a way to represent parts of a whole using a base-10 system, similar to whole numbers. It uses a decimal point (".") to separate the whole number part from the fractional part.

- The digits to the **left** of the decimal point represent the whole numbers.
- The digits to the **right** of the decimal point represent fractional parts, where each digit has a place value based on its distance from the decimal point.
    - The digit closest to the decimal point represents tenths (1/10).
    - The digit to its right represents hundredths (1/100).
    - This pattern continues with thousandths (1/1000), ten thousandths (1/10000), and so on.

There are two main types of decimals:

1. Terminating Decimals:

- These decimals have a finite number of digits after the decimal point. The decimal representation eventually ends.
- Example: 2.5 (two and five-tenths)

2. Non-Terminating Decimals:

- These decimals have an infinite number of digits after the decimal point. The digits may repeat in a specific pattern (recurring decimals) or not repeat at all (non-repeating decimals).
  - **Recurring decimals:** These decimals have a block of digits that repeats endlessly. A line is placed above the repeating block to indicate the pattern.
    - Example: 0.3333... (three repeating forever, can also be written as 1/3)
  - **Non-repeating decimals:** These decimals have an infinite number of digits that never repeat in a predictable pattern.
    - Example: Pi ($\pi \approx 3.14159...$), the square root of 2 ($\sqrt{2} \approx 1.41421...$)

Understanding decimals allows us to represent precise measurements and quantities that cannot be expressed as whole numbers or simple fractions.

Learn Decimal Numbers with Rhyme

A whole apple, round and red,
One delicious treat, instead,
But what if we share, with a friend so true?
Cut it in half, there's decimal for you!
Point five, oh five, a number so neat,
Half of the apple, a yummy sweet treat.
Decimal numbers, with a point so fine,

Show us the parts, in a number line.
Look at the cake, with frosting so white,
Cut into slices, a delightful sight.
Three point seven five, a number so tall,
More than three slices, enjoyed by all!
This decimal magic, don't you despair,
Tells us the leftover, a tiny share.
Seven and five hundredths, a piece so small,
Decimals help us measure it all.
Repeating numbers, a special kind,
Three, three, three, forever you'll find.
Like a bouncing ball, it never ends,
A fraction disguised, a decimal friend.
Pi (π) comes next, a mystery untold,
Its decimal places, forever unfold.
Non-repeating numbers, a twist in the tale,
Digits go on, without ever a fail.
So decimals help us, with parts so small,
From tiny cookies, to planets so tall.
Terminating or repeating, they all have a place,
Numbers with a point, in a magical race!

Chapter 9: The Cryptic Message on the Wall

◈ **Plot:** They reach the hidden location and find a cryptic message on the wall with coded percentages.

◈ **Defining Number:** Percentages

◈ **Activities:** Calculating percentages, solving problems involving discounts and markups.

◈ **Tips & Tricks:** Relate percentages to parts of a hundred, use proportion problems to solve for percentages.

The pressure was on!

Maya and Ben worked together like a well-oiled machine, deciphering the messages on the screen with lightning speed. Each cryptic message, translated through their knowledge of decimals, revealed a specific task – climb a certain number of steps, spin a hidden wheel a designated number of times, or decipher a symbol puzzle within a limited timeframe.

With seconds ticking away on the timer, they completed each challenge with impressive teamwork. Finally, with a triumphant beep, the timer reached zero, and a hidden door creaked open beside the park bench.

Stepping through the doorway, Maya and Ben found themselves in a dimly lit chamber. A single spotlight illuminated a large stone wall covered in strange symbols and swirling patterns. But what truly caught their eye was a series of numbers written in bold font, each followed by a percent sign – 25%, 70%, and 15%.

"Percentages!"

Ben exclaimed, his voice filled with both excitement and confusion.

"What do they have to do with this cryptic message?"

Maya, ever the optimist, grinned. "Maybe they're the key to decoding the symbols on the wall!

Remember how percentages represent parts of a whole?

Maybe we need to find specific sections of the wall based on these percentages!"

Percentages?

A new challenge emerged!

Could understanding percentages be the key to deciphering the cryptic message on the wall?

Calling all math detectives!
Here's your mission:

- **Percentage Puzzle:** Look at the percentages written on the wall (25%, 70%, and 15%). Imagine the entire wall as a whole (100%). Can you identify specific sections of the wall that correspond to each percentage?
- **Symbol Sleuths:** Once you've identified the sections based on percentages, take a closer look at the symbols within those areas. Do the symbols seem to form a pattern or message?

By mastering percentages and using your observation skills, you can help Maya and Ben crack the code on the wall and unlock the next secret in this thrilling mystery!

Remember, percentages are a way to express a part of a whole out of one hundred. Use your math skills and detective instincts to decipher the message and see what awaits them next!

Let Us Learn About Percentage

A percentage is a special way of expressing a part of a whole out of one hundred. It signifies a proportion or ratio, but instead of being written as a fraction or decimal, it's written as a number followed by a percent sign "%".

Here's the breakdown:

- **100% represents the whole**: This means everything or all of something.
- **A percentage less than 100% represents a part of the whole**: The lower the percentage, the smaller the part it represents.
- **A percentage greater than 100% represents more than the whole**: This is uncommon but can be used in specific contexts, like exceeding a target by 120%.

Here are some examples of percentages:

- **50%** - This means half (one out of two) or 50 out of 100 parts. You might get 50% on a test, meaning you answered half the questions correctly.
- **25%** - This represents a quarter (one out of four) or 25 out of 100 parts. You might get a 25% discount on an item, which means the price is reduced by a quarter of its original value.
- **120%** - This indicates exceeding the whole by 20%. For example, a company might achieve 120% of its sales target, meaning they sold 20% more than what they aimed for.

Learn Percentage with Rhyme

A whole pie cut up, a yummy delight,
One hundred slices, what a glorious sight!
Percent comes in, to help us see,
How much of the pie, belongs to you and me.
Fifty percent, a number so neat,
Half of the pie, a sugary treat!
Fifty out of a hundred, a fair share to hold,
Percentage magic, a story untold.
Twenty-five percent, a smaller slice,
One out of four, a delicious price.
Twenty-five slices, for a friend so true,
Sharing the pie, with percentages too.
Seventy-five percent, a number quite grand,
Three out of four slices, in your happy hand.
Seventy-five out of a hundred, a generous part,
Percentage portions, warming your heart.
One hundred percent, the whole pie complete,
All the slices gathered, a sugary feat!
A full circle of flavor, a perfect display,

Percentages help us measure, in a yummy way!
So next time you see a percent sign,
Don't you fret or unwind.
It's just a part, of a bigger surprise,
A number game, with delicious pies!

Chapter 10: Cracking the Coded Lock

◇ **Plot:** The cryptic message reveals the combination for a coded lock using percentages.

◇ **Activities:** Devise their own coded messages using percentages, practice using a combination lock based on percentages.

◇ **Tips & Tricks:** Break down percentages into fractions or decimals for easier calculations.

Following their hunch about percentages, Maya and Ben stood before the mysterious wall, their eyes scanning the swirling symbols. They remembered the numbers – 25%, 70%, and 15% – and how these numbers might represent specific sections of the wall.

Using their knowledge of percentages, they meticulously divided the wall into sections. 25% of the wall was a significant portion on the left, marked by a faint crack in the stone. 70% of the wall spanned most of the remaining space, leaving a final 15% section on the right.

Intriguingly, each section seemed to have its own unique set of symbols. The leftmost section (25%) displayed a series of geometric shapes – triangles, squares, and circles. The middle section (70%) was adorned with various letters of the alphabet, seemingly scrambled and out of order. Finally, the rightmost section (15%) held a sequence of numbers, ranging from 1 to 10.

"These symbols seem to be different in each section," Maya observed, her voice filled with curiosity.

"Do you think they might be parts of a message?"

Ben, his eyes glued to the jumble of letters in the middle section, gasped in realization. "Wait a minute, Maya!

Look at the letters!"

He pointed excitedly at the central section. "If you rearrange these letters based on their position within the 70% section, they actually spell a word – COMBINATION!"

A thrill shot through Maya. "Combination!

That must be the key to unlocking something!"

Their eyes darted to the remaining sections – the geometric shapes and the sequence of numbers. Could these be the actual combination they needed?

Calling all math detectives!

Here's your mission:

- **Combination Challenge:** Remember the percentages (25%, 70%, and 15%) and how they divided the wall. Look at the symbols within each section – the geometric shapes (left section – 25%), the scrambled letters (middle section – 70%), and the number sequence (right section – 15%).

- **Codebreaker Countdown:** Can you use the information gleaned from each section to decipher the combination for the coded lock? Maybe the geometric shapes represent a specific order, the rearranged letters spell out a clue, and the number sequence provides the actual numbers for the combination.

By combining your knowledge of percentages, observation skills, and a dash of logic, you can help Maya and Ben crack the coded lock and finally uncover the secret hidden behind the mysterious wall!

Remember, use the clues from each section based on their size (determined by the percentages) to form a complete combination for the lock.

Chapter 11: The Baffling Balance Scales

◇ **Plot:** Behind the unlocked door, they find a room with two balance scales and coded weights on various objects.

◇ **Defining Number:** Ratios

◇ **Activities:** Setting up balance scales, solving ratio problems to find missing weights or quantities based on the coded clues.

◇ **Tips & Tricks:** Relate ratios to comparisons between two quantities, use visuals to represent ratios.

Relief washed over Maya and Ben as the satisfying click of the unlocked door echoed through the chamber. Stepping inside, they found themselves in a dimly lit room filled with an assortment of curious objects – antique clocks, dusty books, and a strange contraption with two hanging scales.

But what truly captured their attention were the objects placed on each scale pan. Each object had a small sticker with a peculiar symbol and a string of numbers attached to it.

"What's going on here?"

Ben scratched his head, a puzzled look on his face. "Are these some kind of weird weights?"

Maya, ever the detective, crouched down to examine the objects and their corresponding stickers. "Maybe they are weights," she mused, "but the numbers next to them look strange. They have colons separating them, like this: 2:3."

A spark of recognition flickered in Ben's eyes. "Wait a minute, Maya!

Remember learning about ratios in math class?

Maybe these numbers represent ratios between the weights of the objects!"

Ratios?

A new challenge presented itself!

Could understanding ratios be the key to solving the puzzle of the balancing scales?

Calling all math detectives!

Here's your mission:

- **Ratio Reasoning:** Look at the objects on the scales and the stickers with the numbers separated by colons (e.g., 2:3). These numbers represent the ratio between the weights of the two objects being compared. For example, 2:3 might mean that the object on the left-hand side weighs 2 parts, while the object on the right weighs 3 parts.

- **Balancing Bonanza:** Now that you understand the ratios, analyze the objects on each scale pan. Can you adjust the position of the objects (or add/remove objects from a nearby table with similar objects) to ensure that the weights on each side of the scale balance each other out according to the given ratios?

By using your knowledge of ratios and critical thinking skills, you can help Maya and Ben solve the balancing scale puzzle!

Remember, ratios compare the sizes or quantities of two things. Use your math skills and logic to achieve perfect balance on each scale, and see what awaits them on the other side!

Let Us Learn About Ratios And Its Types

A ratio is a mathematical expression that compares the sizes of two quantities of the same kind. It represents the **proportion** between them and tells you how much of one quantity there is for every unit of the other quantity. Ratios can be written in a few different ways:

- **Colon (:)** - This is the most common way to express a ratio. For example, 3:2 represents a ratio of 3 to 2.

- **Fraction** - A ratio can be written as a fraction, where the numerator represents the first quantity and the denominator represents the second quantity. So, 3:2 can also be written as 3/2.

- **Words** - Sometimes, ratios can be expressed in words, like "3 to 2" or "for every 3 apples, there are 2 oranges."

Here are the different types of ratios:

- **Part-to-whole ratio:** This type of ratio compares a part of something to the whole thing.
    - Example: In a class of 20 students, if 8 students have brown hair, the ratio of students with brown hair to the total number of students is 8:20. This can also be written as 2:5, since dividing both sides by 4 keeps the proportion the same.
- **Part-to-part ratio:** This type of ratio compares two parts of a whole.
    - Example: If there are 10 red apples and 6 green apples in a basket, the ratio of red apples to green apples is 10:6.

Important points to remember about ratios:

- Ratios only compare quantities of the same kind. You cannot compare apples and oranges directly using a ratio.
- You can simplify ratios by dividing the numerator and denominator by the greatest common factor (GCD) as long as the GCD is not zero.
- Ratios can be used to solve proportion problems, where you set up two ratios that are equivalent (equal to each other).

Learn Ratios And Its Types with Rhyme

Red socks and blue, in a drawer so deep,

Five red socks there, and three blue to keep.
A ratio tale, to help us see,
How many of each, a mystery!
Five to three, that's the way it goes,
For every five red socks, three blue ones compose.
A colon splits them, a fraction's disguise,
Ratios help us compare, in a counting surprise.
Cookies we bake, a yummy delight,
Two cups of flour, to one cup so white.
A part-to-whole ratio, don't you despair,
Two of flour, for every one sugar to share.
Lemonade stand, with a thirst-quenching dream,
Three cups of water, for one of lemon so keen.
Part-to-part ratio, a balancing act,
Sweet and refreshing, a delicious pact.
So next time you compare, things big or small,
Ratios help you, to answer the call.
From socks in a drawer, to treats we adore,
Ratios help us measure, forevermore!

Chapter 12: The Race Against Time

Rates to the Rescue!

◇ **Plot:** The weights reveal a hidden message about a time-sensitive mission to stop the culprit from escaping.

◇ **Defining Number:** Rates

◇ **Activities:** Calculating rates (e.g., speed, distance/time), solving problems involving rates to determine the culprit's travel time.

◇ **Tips & Tricks:** Break down rate problems into separate steps (distance, time) before calculating the rate.

Sweat beaded on Maya and Ben's foreheads as they meticulously adjusted the objects on the balancing scales. Each object, with its cryptic ratio sticker, presented a unique challenge. But fueled by determination and their newfound understanding of ratios, they managed to achieve perfect balance on both scales with a satisfying clunk.

As the final object settled onto its designated pan, a hidden compartment clicked open beneath one of the scales, revealing a small, rolled-up piece of paper. Relief mixed with anticipation as Maya carefully unfurled it.

"It's a message!"

Ben exclaimed, peering over her shoulder.

But this message was unlike any they had encountered before. It spoke of a "dastardly villain" about to escape with a giant cookie catapult (yes, you read that right!) and a truckload of cookies. The message also mentioned a specific time – 3:15 PM – when the villain's escape was planned.

"We have to stop them!" Maya declared, her voice filled with urgency. "But 3:15 PM is only ten minutes away!"

Suddenly, a phrase from the message jumped out at them: "The villain travels at a rate of 50 kilometers per hour."

Rates?

A new element entered the equation!

Could understanding rates be the key to stopping the villain's cookie heist?

Calling all math detectives!
Here's your mission:

- **Rate Reasoning:** Look at the information about the villain's travel speed – 50 kilometers per hour. Remember, rate refers to the speed or change of something over time (in this case, distance traveled in one hour).

- **Time Trial Triumph:** Since you know the villain's escape time (3:15 PM) and their travel rate (50 kilometers per hour), can you estimate how far the villain might have traveled by that time? This might help you determine the location where they might be setting up their cookie catapult!

By using your knowledge of rates and thinking quickly, you can help Maya and Ben locate the villain and put a stop to their cookie-fueled crimes!

Remember, rates tell you how fast something is happening (speed) or changing (like distance traveled over time). Use your math skills and detective instincts to catch the villain before it's too late for the cookies!

Let Us Learn About Rates And Its Types

A rate refers to the relationship between two **different quantities** measured in **different units** that change over time. It expresses how much of one quantity occurs in relation to the change in another quantity. Rates are often used to describe speed, change, or flow.

Here are some key points about rates:

- **Units:** Rates always involve two units, one for each quantity being compared. For example, speed is expressed in miles per hour (mph) or kilometers per hour (km/h).

- **Change over time:** Rates typically involve a change in one quantity over a specific time interval. For example, a rate of water flow might be gallons per minute (gpm).

- **Types of rates:** There are many different types of rates used in various contexts. Here are a few common examples:

- ○ **Speed:** This is the rate at which an object changes its position over time. It can be expressed in miles per hour (mph), kilometers per hour (km/h), feet per second (fps), etc.
- ○ **Price rate:** This refers to the cost per unit of something. Examples include dollars per gallon (for gasoline), cents per pound (for apples), etc.
- ○ **Interest rate:** This is the percentage charged on a loan or earned on an investment over a specific period. It's usually expressed as a yearly rate (annual percentage rate - APR).
- ○ **Work rate:** This measures how much work is done per unit of time. It could be items produced per hour, pages read per minute, etc.

Here are some examples of rates with explanations:

- **A car travels 100 miles in 2 hours.** The rate is 50 miles per hour (mph) because 100 miles / 2 hours = 50 mph.
- **Oranges cost $2.50 per pound.** This is a price rate indicating the cost per unit (pound) of oranges.
- **A faucet leaks at a rate of 3 drops per second.** This describes the flow rate of the leak.

Learn Rates And Its Types with Rhyme

A cheetah sprints fast, a blur on the plains,
How fast it travels, removes all the pains.
Seventy miles per hour, a speedy rate,
The distance it covers, can't wait to calculate!
Rate's the connection, of things that change,
Like miles and hours, in a re-arranging.
Speed of a bike, or a dripping hose,
Rates tell the story, wherever it goes.
Price at the store, for apples so round,
Two dollars a pound, the best deal in town.
A rate tells the value, for things big or small,

Price per unit, a magical call.
Baking a cake, with flour so white,
Three cups in ten minutes, a mixing delight.
Work rate we see, how much gets done,
The amount completed, under the sun.
So next time you wonder, how fast or how much,
Rates come to help you, with a magic touch.
From cheetahs that race, to cakes in the oven,
Rates show the changes, a never-ending lovin'!

Chapter 13: The Encrypted Phone Message

◇ **Plot:** They receive a coded phone message with instructions requiring them to decipher negative numbers.

◇ **Defining Number:** Negative Numbers

◇ **Activities:** Representing negative numbers on a number line, solving addition and subtraction problems involving negative numbers.

◇ **Tips & Tricks:** Use real-world examples (e.g., temperature below zero) to understand negative numbers.

Just as Maya and Ben were about to jump on their bikes and chase after the cookie-loving villain, a loud ring pierced the air. Maya fumbled for her phone – it was an unknown number.

"Hello?" she answered cautiously.

A distorted voice crackled through the receiver. "Listen carefully, little detectives. You've gotten close, but you'll never stop my cookie caper!

To find the catapult's location, head to the park entrance at coordinates (-3, 7). But beware, these coordinates are trickier than they seem..."

With a mischievous chuckle, the call ended abruptly. Disappointment washed over Maya, but Ben's eyes gleamed with newfound determination.

"Coordinates with negative numbers?" he exclaimed. "That must be another clue!"

Negative Numbers?

This unexpected twist threw a curveball at their mission!

Could negative numbers be the key to deciphering the villain's cryptic message?

Calling all math detectives!

Here's your mission:

- **Negative Number Navigation:** The villain mentioned coordinates with negative numbers (-3, 7). In math, negative numbers represent values less than zero. Imagine a map where zero represents the center point. Points to the right and up from zero would have positive coordinates, while points to the left and down from zero would have negative coordinates.

- **Codebreaker Countdown:** Using your understanding of negative numbers, can you interpret the coordinates (-3, 7) provided in the phone message? This will lead you to the specific location (park entrance) where you need to go next!

By using your knowledge of negative numbers and map reading skills, you can help Maya and Ben decipher the villain's message and get one step closer to stopping their cookie crime spree!

Remember, negative numbers indicate positions to the left or below a central point (zero) on a map-like coordinate system. Use your math skills and detective instincts to pinpoint the park entrance location based on these coordinates!

Let Us Learn About Integers And Its Types

Integers are a set of whole numbers that include zero, positive whole numbers, and their negative counterparts. They represent whole quantities, positive or negative, but not fractions or decimals. Here's a breakdown:

- **Whole Numbers:** These are natural numbers (counting numbers) starting from 1 and going on infinitely, along with zero (0). They represent whole objects and are not fractions or decimals. Examples: 0, 1, 2, 3, 4, 5...

- **Integers:** They encompass whole numbers and extend their range by including their negatives. So, integers include negative whole numbers, zero, and positive whole numbers. Examples: -5, -4, -3, 0, 1, 2, 3...

There are no specific types of integers within the number system itself. However, depending on the context or mathematical operation, integers can be categorized based on their properties:

- **Positive Integers:** These are whole numbers greater than zero. Examples: 1, 2, 3, 4, 5...
- **Negative Integers:** These are whole numbers less than zero. Examples: -1, -2, -3, -4, -5...
- **Even Integers:** These are integers that are divisible by 2 with no remainder. Examples: -10, -6, -4, 0, 2, 4, 6, 8...
- **Odd Integers:** These are integers that leave a remainder of 1 when divided by 2. Examples: -9, -7, -5, -3, 1, 3, 5, 7...

It's important to remember that integers are distinct from other number types like:

- **Natural Numbers:** These are only positive whole numbers (1, 2, 3, ...) and do not include zero or negative numbers.
- **Rational Numbers:** These numbers can be expressed as a fraction where the numerator and denominator are integers (denominator cannot be zero). They represent parts of a whole or ratios between quantities. Examples: 1/2, 3/4, -5/7.
- **Irrational Numbers:** These numbers cannot be expressed as a simple fraction. Their decimal representation never ends or repeats in a predictable pattern. Examples: Pi ($\pi \approx 3.14159$), the square root of 2 ($\sqrt{2} \approx 1.41421$).

Learn Integers And Its Types with Rhyme

Integers come, a counting crew,
Whole numbers positive, and brand new!
Zero joins the fun, a starting place,
Counting up and down, a happy chase.

One little seed, two leaves so green,
Three juicy apples, a yummy scene.
These are whole numbers, happy and bold,
Integers include them, a story untold.
Positive numbers, reaching high,
Four in the clouds, way up in the sky.
Five bouncy balls, a joyful band,
Integers welcome them, a helping hand.
But wait there's more, a twist in the tale,
Numbers below zero, a number trail.
Negative six, a chilly breeze,
Integers include these, if you please!
Even numbers marching, two by two,
Eight friendly penguins, greeting you.
Ten cuddly kittens, in a purring line,
Even integers, perfectly aligned.
Odd numbers standing out, so bright,
One lonely sock, lost in the night.
Three different candies, a colorful treat,
Odd integers, never miss a beat.
So integers teach us, with a happy song,
Counting up and down, where we belong.
Positive, negative, even and odd,
A number family, never a clod!

Chapter 14: The Geometric Gateway

◇ **Plot:** The phone message leads them to a building with a geometric gateway requiring calculations to unlock.

◇ **Defining Number:** Geometry (Area & Perimeter)

◇ **Activities:** Calculating the area and perimeter of shapes (squares, rectangles) based on coded measurements.

◇ **Tips & Tricks:** Use formulas for area and perimeter, visualize the shapes to understand the calculations.

Following the decoded coordinates from the phone message, Maya and Ben raced towards the park entrance. Their hearts pounded with anticipation – could this be where the villain was hiding their cookie catapult?

As they burst through the park gates, a peculiar sight greeted them. Standing in the center of a clearing was a magnificent archway, unlike anything they had ever seen before. It seemed to be constructed from a series of colorful geometric shapes – squares, triangles, and circles – all perfectly interlocked.

But blocking their path was a shimmering force field emanating from the archway. Embedded within the geometric design were panels displaying cryptic symbols and numbers.

"This must be the entrance to the villain's lair!"

Ben exclaimed, his voice filled with excitement. "But how do we get through?"

Maya, ever the observant one, pointed at the panels. "Look!

There are shapes and numbers on these panels. Maybe they're some kind of geometric puzzle!"

Geometry?

A new challenge loomed before them!

Could their knowledge of geometry, specifically area and perimeter, be the key to unlocking the geometric gateway?

Calling all math detectives!

Here's your mission:

- **Geometric Genius:** Look closely at the panels on the gateway. You'll see various geometric shapes (squares, triangles, circles) with numbers next to them. These numbers might represent measurements like side lengths or radii.

- **Perimeter Prowess & Area Analysis:** Remember what you know about area (the space occupied by a flat shape) and perimeter (the total distance around the outside of a shape). Can you use the measurements provided (numbers next to the shapes) to calculate the area or perimeter of each geometric shape displayed on the panels?

- **Unlocking the Gateway:** Maybe the calculated areas or

perimeters are the key to unlocking the gateway. Look for patterns or relationships between the calculations and the symbols on the panels. Could these values be used to activate specific panels or enter a code to deactivate the force field?

By using your knowledge of geometry, specifically area and perimeter calculations, and your critical thinking skills, you can help Maya and Ben unlock the geometric gateway and confront the villain behind the cookie caper!

Remember, use the measurements provided to calculate the area or perimeter of each shape, and see if these values can help deactivate the force field or reveal the correct sequence to unlock the gateway.

Let Us Learn About Area And Perimeter

Area and perimeter are both important concepts used to measure different aspects of a flat shape (two-dimensional shape). Here's a breakdown of each:

Area:

- The area of a flat shape refers to the amount of space the entire shape occupies.
- It represents the surface covered by the shape, measured in square units (square centimeters, square inches, square meters, etc.).
- Imagine the shape filled with a thin layer of material, like paper or fabric. The area tells you how much of that material you would need to cover the entire shape completely.

Example:

- Consider a rectangle with a length of 5 centimeters (cm) and a width of 3 cm. To find the area, we multiply the length by the width: Area = length x width = 5 cm x 3 cm = 15 square centimeters (sq cm). This means you would need a square piece of paper with sides 15 cm long to cover the entire rectangle.

Perimeter:

- The perimeter of a flat shape refers to the total length of all its sides added together.
- It represents the complete outer boundary or "fence" around the shape, measured in linear units (centimeters, inches, meters, etc.).
- Imagine walking around the entire shape following its edges. The perimeter tells you the total distance you would walk.

Example:

- Using the same rectangle with a length of 5 cm and a width of 3 cm, the perimeter would be: Perimeter = total length of all sides. Since there are two long sides of 5 cm each and two short sides of 3 cm each, we add them all up: Perimeter = 2 x 5 cm + 2 x 3 cm = 10 cm + 6 cm = 16 centimeters (cm). So, the total distance you would walk around the entire rectangle is 16 cm.

Key Difference:

- Area measures the **space** occupied by the shape, while perimeter measures the **total length** of its boundary.
- Area is measured in square units, while perimeter is measured in linear units.

Learn Area And Perimeter with Rhyme

A garden so green, with flowers so bright,
Let's measure the space, with all our might!
Area's the word, for the space it will hold,

Like a blanket so cozy, keeping flowers from the cold.
Square feet or square inches, the units we choose,
To measure the ground, for all the blooms to use.
Length times width, a simple delight,
The area we find, what a beautiful sight!
A rectangular pond, with fish swimming free,
Let's measure the edges, around you and me!
Perimeter's turn, to hold all the fun,
The total distance, around everyone!
Adding the sides, up and down we go,
Length plus length, plus width, in a happy flow.
The distance we walk, around the whole pond,
Perimeter's magic, a never-ending bond.
So area tells us, the space a shape claims,
While perimeter whispers, the length of its frames.
One measures the inside, a colorful quest,
The other the outside, where walking is best!

Chapter 15: The Coded Security Camera Footage

Elapsed Time to the Rescue

◈ **Plot:** Inside the building, they find coded timestamps on security camera footage to identify the culprit.

◈ **Defining Number:** Elapsed Time

◈ **Activities:** Solving problems involving elapsed time (start time, end time, duration) based on the coded timestamps.

◈ **Tips & Tricks:** Draw timelines to represent the coded timestamps and calculate the elapsed time.

With a triumphant whoosh, the shimmering force field around the geometric gateway deactivated, granting Maya and Ben access to the hidden lair behind it. Relief washed over them, but a sense of urgency lingered. They had to stop the villain before their cookie heist came to fruition!

Stepping inside, they found themselves in a large, brightly lit room filled with all sorts of machinery and, more importantly, countless boxes of cookies stacked high in the corner. But the room was eerily silent.

Suddenly, a flicker of movement on a nearby monitor caught their eye. It was a security camera feed, but the timestamps seemed strange – instead of displaying regular clock times, they showed a series of numbers followed by the letters "ET."

"What's ET?"

Ben scratched his head, a confused look on his face.

"Maybe it's not extraterrestrial this time," Maya mused, tapping her chin thoughtfully. "Remember how we used elapsed time to figure out the library book?"

Elapsed Time?

A spark of recognition flickered in their eyes!

Could elapsed time be the key to deciphering the timestamps on the security camera footage?

Calling all math detectives!

Here's your mission:

- **Elapsed Time Escapades:** Look at the timestamps on the security camera footage. They display numbers followed by the letters "ET," which likely stands for "elapsed time." Remember, elapsed time refers to the total time that has passed between a starting point and an ending point.

- **Footage Frenzy:** Since you don't have a starting point (a specific time when the recording began), focus on the differences between the timestamps. Can you calculate the elapsed time between different events captured on camera?
- **Identifying the Imposter:** The security footage might show various people entering and leaving the lair throughout the day. By calculating the elapsed time between their entries and exits, can you identify any suspicious activity and potentially unmask the culprit behind the cookie caper?

By using your knowledge of elapsed time and analyzing the security camera footage, you can help Maya and Ben identify the villain and put a stop to their plans before they escape with a truckload of cookies!

Remember, elapsed time is the total duration between an event's start and finish. Use your math skills and detective instincts to analyze the time differences and identify the culprit in the footage!

Let Us Learn About Elapsed Time

Elapsed time refers to the **duration** that has passed between a starting point and an ending point in a specific event or process. It's the **total time** taken for something to happen.

Here are some key points about elapsed time:

- It's always measured in **positive units** like seconds, minutes, hours, days, years, etc.
- Elapsed time is independent of the speed or pace at which something happens. It only focuses on the total duration from start to finish.
- We can calculate elapsed time by subtracting the starting time from the ending time.

Example:

Imagine a movie starts at 7:00 PM and ends at 9:15 PM. To find the elapsed time of the movie, we subtract the starting time from the ending time:

Elapsed time = Ending time - Starting time Elapsed time = 9:15 PM - 7:00 PM

Since we're dealing with time within the same day, we can simply subtract the hours and minutes:

Elapsed time = 2 hours 15 minutes

Therefore, the movie has an elapsed time of 2 hours and 15 minutes.

Learn Elapsed Time with Rhyme

The clock strikes ten, the race begins,
Five minutes fly, like papery pins.
Elapsed time whispers, the time that's gone,
From ten o'clock, to tick-tock's dawn.
Cookies in the oven, a yummy delight,
Ten minutes to bake, until golden and bright.
Elapsed time watches, the minutes they fly,
Taking us closer, to that warm, gooey pie!
A movie marathon, with friends so dear,
Three hours we watch, with laughter and cheer.
Elapsed time counts them, the moments that zoom,
An afternoon filled, erasing the gloom.
Sunrise to sunset, a glorious sight,
Twelve hours have passed, day turns into night.
Elapsed time measures, the journey of light,
From morning's first peek, to the starry night.
So next time you wonder, how long it will be,
Elapsed time's magic, sets your mind free.
From cookies to movies, or the sun's golden ray,
It tells us the duration, in a delightful way!

Chapter 16: The Logical Reasoning Labyrinth

◈ **Plot:** After reviewing the security footage, they find a hidden door with a series of cryptic riddles requiring logical reasoning skills.

◈ **Defining Number:** Not directly a number type, but uses logic and critical thinking.

◈ **Activities:** Solving logic puzzles, identifying patterns and inconsistencies in the riddles, using deduction to reach conclusions.

◈ **Tips & Tricks:** Break down the riddles step-by-step, identify key words and clues, consider all possibilities before reaching a conclusion.

Heartbeats pounding with anticipation, Maya and Ben scrutinized the security camera footage. Each elapsed time they calculated revealed a piece of the puzzle. Finally, after careful analysis, they noticed a suspicious figure entering the lair shortly before the message about the cookie catapult.

"That must be the villain!"

Ben exclaimed, pointing at the screen.

But just as they were about to confront the culprit, a hidden compartment within the room whirred open, revealing a final challenge – a heavy metal door secured by a series of locks.

Etched onto the door were not numbers or symbols, but a series of riddles. These riddles, however, didn't involve any calculations. They tested something different – logical reasoning and critical thinking skills.

Logical Reasoning?

A brand new challenge emerged!

This wasn't about numbers or calculations, but about using logic and critical thinking to solve puzzles.

Calling all math detectives, and now logic puzzlers!

Here's your mission:

- **Riddle Racers:** Read each riddle carefully. These riddles will test your ability to analyze information, identify patterns, and draw logical conclusions.
- **Reasoning Revelation:** By using your critical thinking skills and logic, can you solve each riddle and determine the mechanism to unlock the corresponding lock on the metal door?

- **Confronting the Culprit:** Once you've solved all the riddles and unlocked the door, Maya and Ben can finally confront the villain behind the cookie caper!

By using your logical reasoning skills and thinking creatively, you can help Maya and Ben solve the riddles, unlock the final door, and bring this cookie caper to a satisfying conclusion!

Remember, these riddles won't require complex math calculations, but rather your sharp mind and ability to think critically to solve them and reach the villain!

Chapter 17: Coded Measurements

⬦ **Plot:** The riddles lead them to a hidden passage with coded measurements for length, width, and height.

⬦ **Defining Number:** Units of Measurement (meters, litres, grams)

⬦ **Activities:** Converting between different units of measurement (e.g., centimeters to meters) based on the coded clues, using measuring tools to verify their calculations.

⬦ **Tips & Tricks:** Use a conversion chart to keep track of different units, visualize the measurements to understand the scale.

With a chorus of clicks and whirs, the final lock on the metal door yielded to their brilliant deductions. Maya and Ben exchanged a triumphant grin – they were finally about to confront the mastermind behind the great cookie caper!

Pushing open the heavy door, they were greeted with a dark and narrow passage. A single flickering lantern cast an eerie glow on the rough-hewn stone walls.

"This must be the secret entrance to the villain's lair!"

Maya whispered, a shiver of excitement running down her spine.

As they ventured deeper into the passage, their eyes adjusted to the dim light, revealing strange markings etched onto the walls. These markings weren't riddles or symbols, but rather a series of numbers accompanied by unfamiliar abbreviations – "m," "L," and "g."

"What are these numbers?"

Ben furrowed his brow, his voice barely a whisper in the silent passage.

"Maybe they're measurements," Maya chimed in, her mind racing. "But what do the letters stand for?"

Units of Measurement?

A new twist presented itself!

These unfamiliar abbreviations could be the key to navigating the secret passage.

Calling all math detectives!

Here's your mission:

- **Measurement Mania:** Look closely at the numbers and abbreviations on the walls (m, L, and g). These likely represent measurements of length, volume, and weight, but in unfamiliar units.

- **Unit Equation Experts:** While you might not be familiar with "m," "L," and "g" in this context, you do know about common units of measurement like meters (m) for length, litres (L) for volume, and grams (g) for weight. Can you analyze the values and abbreviations together to form a logical connection between them?
- **Maze Navigation:** Imagine the measurements represent the dimensions (length, width, and height) of different sections of the passage. By using your understanding of units and the values provided, can you determine which direction to walk in the passage to reach the villain's lair?

By using your knowledge of measurement units and critical thinking skills, you can help Maya and Ben decipher the coded measurements, navigate the secret passage, and finally come face-to-face with the culprit!

Remember, analyze the measurements and abbreviations together to make sense of the units and navigate the passage based on the dimensions provided.

Let Us Learn About Units of Measurement And Its Type

A unit of measurement is a standardized reference point used to express the quantity of a physical property. It allows us to compare and communicate measurements precisely. There are many different types of units used in various scientific disciplines and everyday life. Here's a breakdown of some common types:

1. Fundamental Units:

These are the basic units from which other units are derived. The International System of Units (SI) defines seven fundamental units:

- **Length:** Meter (m) - The basic unit for measuring distance or length.
- **Mass:** Kilogram (kg) - The basic unit for measuring mass, the

amount of matter in an object.

- **Time:** Second (s) - The basic unit for measuring time.
- **Electric Current:** Ampere (A) - The basic unit for measuring the flow of electric current.
- **Temperature:** Kelvin (K) - The basic unit for measuring temperature on the Kelvin scale.
- **Amount of Substance:** Mole (mol) - The basic unit for measuring the amount of a substance, representing a specific number of particles (atoms, molecules, ions).
- **Luminous Intensity:** Candela (cd) - The basic unit for measuring the intensity of light.

2. Derived Units:

These units are created by combining fundamental units using multiplication, division, or exponentiation. Examples include:

- **Area:** Square meter (m^2) - Derived from multiplying meter by meter (length x width).
- **Volume:** Cubic meter (m^3) - Derived from multiplying meter by meter by meter (length x width x height).
- **Speed:** Meter per second (m/s) - Derived from dividing meter (distance) by second (time).
- **Force:** Newton (N) - Derived from multiplying kilogram (mass) by meter per second squared (acceleration).

3. Other Unit Systems:

Besides the SI system, other unit systems are used in specific contexts. Here are a few examples:

- **Imperial System:** Uses units like inches, feet, miles, pounds, ounces, etc., commonly used in the United States.
- **Metric System:** An older system based on the meter, with

units like centimeters, liters, grams, etc. (largely replaced by SI).

- **US Customary Units:** A mix of units used in the United States for everyday purposes, like gallons for liquids, Fahrenheit for temperature, etc.

Examples of Units in Action:

- We measure the length of a table in meters (m).
- We express the weight of a person in kilograms (kg).
- We cook a recipe that requires a specific amount of time in minutes (min) and oven temperature in degrees Celsius (°C).
- We measure the distance traveled by a car in kilometers per hour (km/h).

Understanding units of measurement is crucial for scientific communication, engineering applications, and everyday tasks that involve measurement and comparison.

Learn Units of Measurement And Its Type with Rhyme

A ruler so long, with markings so neat,
Measures the table, in meters complete.
Units of measure, a helping hand friend,
Tell us how big, or how far it will bend.
Meters for giants, and millimeters so small,
Units come in sizes, to fit everything at all.
Fundamental seven, the building block crew,
Length, mass, and time, a perfect, strong shoe.
From seconds that tick, to kilograms so grand,
These basic units, help us understand.
Derived units join them, a multiplying race,
Area and volume, with a spacial embrace.
Square meters for carpets, and cubes for a box,
Units fit the picture, like socks in their box.

Beyond meters and grams, other systems appear,
Inches and pounds, some things hold them dear.
The US cooks in cups, while Celsius tells heat,
Units have their places, a specialized feat.
So next time you measure, a cake or a tree,
The right unit's the magic, for you and for me!

Chapter 18: Data Analysis

◇ **Plot:** The passage leads to a room filled with coded charts and graphs containing information about the culprit's activities.

◇ **Defining Number:** Data Analysis (interpreting data)

◇ **Activities:** Interpreting data from bar graphs, pie charts, and line graphs, identifying trends and patterns in the coded data.

◇ **Tips & Tricks:** Pay attention to labels and legends on the charts, look for relationships between different data points.

Following the cryptic measurements on the walls, Maya and Ben emerged from the narrow passage into a room unlike any they had seen before. The room was brightly lit, filled with computer screens displaying a jumble of charts, graphs, and tables.

"What is all this?"

Ben exclaimed, overwhelmed by the sheer amount of data.

"It looks like information about the cookie caper!"

Maya gasped, her eyes widening with realization.

Scattered amongst the digital displays were rows of overflowing filing cabinets, their labels marked with cryptic codes.

"This must be the villain's secret data center!"

Ben whispered, a hint of awe in his voice. "But how do we make sense of all this?"

Data Analysis?

A whole new challenge unfolded before them!

This room wasn't guarded by riddles or locks, but by a mountain of coded data. They needed to use their data analysis skills to interpret the information and unmask the culprit.

Calling all math detectives and data analysts!
Here's your mission:

- **Data Detectives:** Look closely at the charts, graphs, and tables displayed on the screens. These visuals likely represent information about the villain's activities, such as cookie types stolen, baking times, and maybe even their preferred method of transportation (remember the cookie catapult?).
- **Information Investigators:** Each chart, graph, and table uses

data (numbers and visuals) to convey information. Can you interpret the information presented in these visuals? Look for patterns, trends, and relationships between the data points.

- **Cracking the Cookie Caper:** By analyzing the data, can you identify any clues that point to the culprit's identity? The data might reveal their cookie preferences, baking habits, or even their escape route!

By using your data analysis skills and critical thinking abilities, you can help Maya and Ben interpret the information in the room, identify the culprit behind the cookie caper, and bring this delicious mystery to a close!

Remember, analyze the data in the charts, graphs, and tables to find patterns and clues that reveal the culprit's identity and plans.

Let Us Learn About Data Analysis And Its Type

Data analysis is the process of inspecting, cleansing, transforming, and modeling data with the goal of discovering useful information, informing conclusions, and supporting decision-making. It's like sifting through a pile of sand to find hidden treasures – the treasures being insights and knowledge hidden within the data.

Here are the four main types of data analysis, each with a different purpose:

1. **Descriptive Analysis:**
    - This is the foundation of data analysis. It focuses on summarizing the data and providing a basic understanding of its characteristics.
    - Techniques used include calculating measures of central tendency (mean, median, mode) and dispersion (range, variance, standard deviation), creating frequency tables, and visualizing the data with charts and graphs (histograms, bar charts, pie

charts).

- **Example:** Analyzing sales data might involve finding the average monthly sales, the most popular product category, and creating charts to see trends over time.

2. **Diagnostic Analysis:**
   - This type of analysis delves deeper, aiming to identify the causes of patterns or trends observed in the data. It explores relationships between variables and tries to explain why things happen the way they do.
   - Techniques used include correlation analysis, regression analysis, and data mining to identify patterns and relationships.
   - **Example:** A company might use diagnostic analysis to understand why customer churn (customers leaving) is happening. They might analyze customer demographics, purchase history, and support interactions to see if any factors correlate with churn.

3. **Predictive Analysis:**
   - This type of analysis uses historical data to build models that can predict future outcomes. It's like using the past to forecast the future.
   - Techniques used include machine learning algorithms, statistical modeling, and forecasting techniques.
   - **Example:** An online store might use predictive analysis to recommend products to customers based on their past purchases and browsing behavior.

4. **Prescriptive Analysis:**

- ◦ This is the most advanced type of analysis. It goes beyond prediction and suggests actions or recommendations based on the insights gained from the data. It helps identify the optimal course of action to achieve a desired outcome.
- ◦ Techniques used include optimization algorithms, simulation modeling, and decision-making frameworks.
- ◦ **Example:** A company might use prescriptive analysis to optimize their marketing campaigns by identifying the most effective channels and target audiences to reach based on customer data.

By using these different types of data analysis, organizations can gain valuable insights from their data, improve decision-making, and achieve their goals.

Learn Data Analysis And Its Type with Rhyme

Data's a mountain, of numbers and facts,
A jumbled up mess, with hidden pacts.
Data analysis, a hero so bright,
Unravels the secrets, and brings them to light.
First comes description, a picture so clear,
Averages and graphs, to banish all fear.
Mean, median, mode, a story they tell,
Of highs and of lows, where the data may dwell.
Diagnostic dives deep, a why and a how,
Relationships sought, with a thoughtful "wow!"
Correlations whisper, a pattern is found,
Explaining the reasons, on data-rich ground.
Predictive whispers, of what might unfold,
Using the past, stories yet untold.
Machine learning magic, a future in sight,

Forecasting the trends, with knowledge and might.
Prescriptive whispers, the best way to go,
Decisions well-guided, a wisdom that flows.
Optimization's magic, a path clear and true,
Using data's insights, to see what to do.
So data analysis, a treasure we find,
From mountains of numbers, a wisdom entwined.
Descriptive, diagnostic, predictive and wise,
Unveiling the stories, that in data arise.

Chapter 19: Probability & Statistics

Statistics Strike Back!

◇ **Plot:** The data analysis reveals the culprit's favorite hiding spots. They need to calculate the probability of finding the culprit at each location.

◇ **Defining Number:** Probability & Statistics (chance and likelihood)

◇ **Activities:** Calculating simple probabilities (e.g., coin toss), using statistics to analyze past patterns and predict future behavior of the culprit.

◇ **Tips & Tricks:** Use probability formulas or simulations (e.g., coin flips) to understand the concept of chance.

With a newfound sense of purpose, Maya and Ben delved into the sea of data on the computer screens. Line graphs depicted rising cookie production rates, bar charts showed the popularity of different cookie flavors, and pie charts revealed the villain's stock of various baking ingredients.

As they analyzed the information, a pattern emerged – the data indicated three potential locations where the culprit might be hiding: the Chocolate Chip Canyon, the Oatmeal Oasis, and the Nutmeg Nook.

"We know the villain's favorite cookies, baking habits, and even their escape vehicle (remember the cookie catapult?)," Maya pointed out. "But which location are they hiding in?"

"There's too much data to guess," Ben chimed in. "We need a way to calculate the chances of finding them at each place!"

Probability & Statistics?

This case required more than just hunches!

They needed the power of statistics and probability to determine the most likely culprit hideout.

Calling all math detectives and data analysts!

Here's your mission:

- **Probability Posse:** Remember, probability refers to the chance of an event happening. In this case, you need to calculate the probability of finding the culprit at each location (Chocolate Chip Canyon, Oatmeal Oasis, and Nutmeg Nook) based on the data you've analyzed.
- **Statistical Sleuths:** The data on the screens likely contains

clues about the villain's preferences for ingredients, baking styles, or even hiding spots. Can you use the data (like favorite cookie types or past hiding spots) to calculate the probability of finding them at each location?

- **Cornering the Cookie Culprit:** By analyzing the data and calculating probabilities, can you determine the location where the culprit is most likely hiding? This will lead Maya and Ben to confront the mastermind behind the cookie caper!

By using your knowledge of probability and statistics, and by critically analyzing the data, you can help Maya and Ben calculate the probability of finding the culprit at each location and apprehend the villain before they escape with their loot!

Remember, use the data provided as clues to calculate the chance of finding the culprit at each spot and identify their most likely hiding place.

Let Us Learn About Probability And Its Type

Probability is the branch of mathematics that deals with the likelihood of events occurring. It expresses the chance or degree of certainty that an event will happen. Probability values range from 0 to 1, where:

- **0** represents an impossible event (certain not to happen).
- **1** represents a certain event (guaranteed to happen).
- Values between 0 and 1 represent the likelihood of the event happening, with higher values indicating a greater chance.

There are three main types of probabilities used to calculate the likelihood of events:

1. **Theoretical Probability:**
    - This type of probability is based on logic and

reasoning, assuming all possible outcomes are equally likely. It's calculated by dividing the number of favorable outcomes (outcomes that satisfy the event) by the total number of possible outcomes.

- **Example:** Flipping a fair coin has two possible outcomes: heads or tails. The theoretical probability of getting heads is 1 favorable outcome (heads) divided by 2 total possible outcomes (heads or tails), resulting in a probability of 1/2 or 50%.

2. **Experimental Probability:**
   - This type of probability is based on observations and data collected from real-world experiments or trials. It's calculated by dividing the number of times the event occurs by the total number of trials conducted.
   - **Example:** Rolling a die and getting a specific number (like a 3) can be tested by rolling the die multiple times and counting how many times you get a 3. The experimental probability would be the number of times you roll a 3 divided by the total number of rolls.

3. **Axiomatic Probability:**
   - This is a more advanced approach based on a set of axioms (fundamental principles) that define the properties of probability. It provides a theoretical framework for probability calculations, especially in complex situations.
   - Understanding the axioms goes beyond the scope of a basic explanation of probability types. However, it's important to know this approach exists.

These three types of probability help us quantify the chance of events happening, allowing us to make informed decisions based on likelihoods rather than just guesses.

Learn Probability And Its Type with Rhyme

Probability's magic, a chance we all face,

The likelihood of something, happening in this space.

From zero to one, the numbers all flow,

Telling a story, of what we may know.

Theoretical whispers, a logical guess,

Equal outcomes dancing, a fair coin to test.

Heads or tails waiting, a fifty-fifty chance,

Probability's magic, in a happy little trance.

Experimental whispers, from trials we see,

Rolling the dice, counting the three.

The more times it happens, the higher the chance,

A real-world approach, given a happy glance.

Axioms come next, a foundation so deep,

The rules of the game, secrets they keep.

Advanced mathematics, a world to explore,

But the basics we learned, will open the door.

So next time you wonder, how likely it might be,

Probability's answer, sets your mind free.

From coins in the air, to games that we play,

It helps us understand, in a wonderful way!

Chapter 20: The Final Showdown

A Math-tastic Conclusion!

◇ **Plot:** Based on probability calculations, they arrive at the culprit's final location and use all their math skills to apprehend them.

◇ **Defining Number:** Review of all math concepts used throughout the story.

◇ **Activities:** Creating a plan that involves various math skills (e.g., calculating distances, using ratios to compare strengths), solving a final math challenge to disable the culprit's escape route.

◇ **Tips & Tricks:** Think creatively and combine all the math skills learned throughout the adventure.

Armed with their knowledge of data analysis, probability, and a healthy dose of determination, Maya and Ben ventured out of the villain's data center. The stolen cookies had to be retrieved, and the culprit brought to justice!

Their statistical calculations pointed to a specific location – The Nutmeg Nook, a secluded area of the park known for its abundance of nutmeg trees, a key ingredient in many of the villain's favorite cookie recipes.

As they approached the Nutmeg Nook, they spotted a suspicious figure hunched over a strange contraption – the cookie catapult!

It was the villain, surrounded by mountains of freshly baked cookies!

But the villain wasn't expecting them.

This was their chance!

In a thrilling display of teamwork and mathematical prowess, Maya and Ben used everything they had learned throughout their adventure:

- **Spotting the Percentages:** Remembering their encounter with percentages on the wall, they quickly devised a plan. Maya noticed several unattended boxes of cookies – 25% chocolate chip, 50% oatmeal raisin, and 25% snickerdoodle.
- **Distraction with Divisibility:** Ben, recalling their lesson on divisibility, shouted out a random number, "Hey! Is that number on your catapult divisible by 3?" Confused by the sudden math question, the villain momentarily glanced at the control panel, creating a crucial window of opportunity.

- **Cracking the Code with Fractions:** In a flash, Maya scrambled towards the catapult. The control panel displayed a cryptic message – a series of fractions like ½ and ¾. Remembering how fractions represented portions, she quickly adjusted the levers accordingly, aiming the catapult upwards and away from the boxes of cookies.
- **A Dash of Decimals:** With a whir and a puff of smoke, the catapult lurched to life, launching a giant cookie dough ball high into the air. But Maya wasn't done yet. Using her knowledge of decimals, she precisely timed a jump, reaching out and grabbing the dough ball mid-air just as it reached its peak (represented by a decimal like 2.5 seconds on an internal timer).
- **Logical Reasoning for the Win:** As the villain sputtered in frustration, Ben tackled them to the ground. With a series of well-reasoned arguments (remember the logical reasoning riddles?), Maya convinced the villain that a life of crime wasn't the answer, and that sharing their delicious cookies was a much better option.

The caper was foiled!

The cookies were saved (well, most of them – the dough ball did land with a splat on the ground), and the villain, after a good talking to about the importance of sharing, decided to use their baking talents for good.

Maya and Ben, exhausted but exhilarated, had not only saved the day, but also solidified their understanding of a whole range of mathematical concepts:

- Divisibility helped them create a distraction.
- Percentages helped them identify the unattended cookie boxes.

- Fractions played a role in controlling the cookie catapult.
- Decimals ensured a perfectly timed jump to catch the dough ball.
- Logical reasoning helped convince the villain to mend their ways.

Their adventure proved that math wasn't just numbers on a page – it was a powerful tool that could be used to solve problems, crack codes, and even save the day (and a whole lot of delicious cookies)!

Chapter 21: The Hidden Motive

A Delicious Twist!

◇ **Plot:** After apprehending the culprit, Maya and Ben delve deeper into the case, uncovering a hidden motive behind the crimes. They discover the culprit wasn't after stealing cookies or causing chaos, but something more personal.

◇ **Defining Number:** Not directly a number type, but may involve calculations depending on the motive (e.g., percentages for a fundraising goal).

With the villain subdued and the cookies (mostly) safe, Maya and Ben took a moment to catch their breath. The mystery of the stolen cookies had been solved, but a nagging question lingered in their minds.

"Why?"

Maya asked, her voice laced with curiosity. "Why would you go through all this trouble to steal cookies?"

The villain, sheepish but strangely relieved, hung their head. "It wasn't about the cookies themselves," they mumbled. "It was about..." they hesitated, then blurted out, "The annual bake-off!"

Intrigued, Maya and Ben exchanged a glance. The annual bake-off was a prestigious event in their town, with awards and bragging rights at stake.

"I've been trying to win for years," the villain confessed, their voice filled with a mixture of sadness and determination. "But no matter how hard I tried, my cookies never seemed to measure up."

A realization dawned on Maya. "So you stole cookies from other bakers to sabotage their entries?"

The villain nodded glumly. "I thought if I got rid of the competition, I might finally have a chance of winning."

Disappointment flickered across Maya and Ben's faces, but it was quickly replaced by understanding. Stealing wasn't the answer, but their desire to win the bake-off was understandable.

"Hey," Ben chimed in, a grin spreading across his face. "Maybe we can help you with that!"

Thus began a new chapter in their adventure. Maya and Ben, along with the remorseful villain (whose name they learned was Charlie), decided to team up for the bake-off.

Over the next few days, their kitchen became a whirlwind of activity. They used their problem-solving skills (honed during their cookie caper) to brainstorm recipe ideas.

- They incorporated Maya's knowledge of ratios to ensure the perfect balance of ingredients in their dough.
- Ben used his understanding of percentages to precisely measure out flour, sugar, and chocolate chips.
- Charlie, eager to prove themself, shared their secret family cookie recipe, a treasure trove of unique flavors and baking techniques.

Finally, the day of the bake-off arrived. The aroma of freshly baked cookies filled the air as Maya, Ben, and Charlie presented their creation – a mouthwatering masterpiece that combined the best of all their skills and knowledge.

As the judges deliberated, a sense of nervous anticipation hung heavy in the air. But when the results were announced, a wave of joy washed over them. Maya, Ben, and Charlie – the former cookie culprit and their newfound math whiz partners – had won the bake-off!

Their victory wasn't just about the trophy or bragging rights. It was a testament to the power of teamwork, collaboration, and of course, a little bit of math magic. They had not only saved the cookies, but also discovered that the sweetest reward wasn't winning, but the joy of baking and sharing together.

Chapter 22: The Power of Teamwork

A Bond Forged in Cookies!

⬦ **Plot:** Maya and Ben realize that their success relies heavily on their teamwork and complementary skills. They reflect on how each other's strengths helped crack the case.

⬦ **Defining Number:** Not directly a number type, but focuses on collaboration.

Exhausted but exhilarated, Maya and Ben sat on a park bench, the golden trophy gleaming between them. Beside them, Charlie beamed, a newfound sense of camaraderie replacing their earlier rivalry.

As they watched the setting sun paint the sky in vibrant hues, a wave of reflection washed over Maya. This adventure had been unlike anything they had ever experienced, filled with puzzles, codes, and of course, a whole lot of cookies.

"We did it," Ben exclaimed, breaking the comfortable silence. "We saved the cookies, outsmarted a villain, and even won the bake-off... all thanks to math!"

Maya nodded, a warm smile gracing her lips. "But it wasn't just math, Ben. It was teamwork.

Remember all those times our different strengths came together?"

Ben chuckled, reminiscing about their journey. "Definitely!

You were the queen of logic, cracking those riddles with ease. And your knowledge of ratios always ensured we had perfectly balanced scales."

"And you, Ben," Maya countered, "your memory for numbers was incredible! You deciphered those coded timestamps on the security footage like a pro."

They continued reminiscing, each highlighting the unique skills the other brought to the table. Maya's meticulous attention to detail and logical reasoning complemented Ben's quick thinking and ability to spot patterns in numbers. Together, they formed a formidable team, capable of solving any mystery that came their way.

Looking towards Charlie, Maya added, "And of course, we couldn't have done it without your secret cookie recipe and baking expertise!"

Charlie grinned sheepishly. "Thanks, guys. You really helped me see the error of my ways. Sharing is definitely more rewarding than stealing."

As the trio watched the last rays of sunlight fade, a sense of deep satisfaction settled in their hearts. Their adventure wasn't just about cookies or trophies. It was about the power of collaboration, about recognizing and appreciating each other's strengths, and about the magic that happens when different minds work together.

They had not only solved a mystery and become baking champions, but they had also forged a bond that was sure to last a lifetime – a bond built on friendship, teamwork, and a shared love for cookies (especially the kind that weren't stolen!).

Chapter 23: The Case of the Curious Code

A Deliciously Encrypted Ending!

◇ **Plot:** Just as Maya and Ben wrap up the case, they discover a hidden message containing a new, unfamiliar code. This sets the stage for a potential sequel adventure.

◇ **Defining Number:** Teaser for future math challenges (introduces a new number concept)

Dipping their well-deserved victory cookies into a shared cup of milk, Maya and Ben chuckled as they recounted their incredible adventure to their wide-eyed friends. The tale of the stolen cookies, the code-breaking challenges, and their teamwork-fueled triumph had them all captivated.

Suddenly, Charlie nudged Maya, a mischievous glint in their eye. "Speaking of codes," they whispered, "remember that strange symbol I found etched on the bottom of the trophy?"

Confused, Maya and Ben exchanged a glance. They had been so caught up in the celebration that they hadn't even noticed. Examining the trophy base, their eyes widened in surprise.

Carved into the smooth metal was a peculiar symbol – a series of interlocking spirals that resembled a seashell. It was unlike any code they had encountered before.

"What do you think it means?"

Ben asked, his voice filled with curiosity.

Charlie shrugged, a playful smile on their face. "Maybe it's a message from another cookie-loving villain," they teased. "Or perhaps a clue to a whole new mystery waiting to be unraveled."

A spark of excitement ignited in Maya's eyes. The thrill of the chase, the challenge of a new code, the prospect of another adventure – it was all too tempting to resist.

"Well, then," Maya declared, a determined glint in her eyes, "I guess we'd better brush up on our code-breaking skills. Because it looks like we have another case on our hands – The Case of the Curious Code!"

The friends erupted in a chorus of cheers, their voices echoing through the park. As the last rays of the setting sun dipped below the horizon, Maya, Ben, and Charlie knew one thing for sure – their adventures with math, cookies, and maybe even a sprinkle of mystery, were far from over.

Chapter 24: Celebrating Success

A Math-tastic Victory!

◇ **Plot:** They celebrate their success, recognizing the importance of math in solving real-world problems.

◇ **Defining Number:** Not directly a number type, but a reflection on the value of math.

◇ **Activities:** Reflect on the different math concepts used throughout the adventure, discuss how math helped them crack the case.

◇ **Tips & Tricks:** Reinforce the importance of math skills for problem-solving and critical thinking.

Victorious and exhausted, Maya, Ben, and Charlie gathered around a table overflowing with their winning cookies. The air buzzed with excitement as they recounted the thrilling moments of their adventure – the coded messages, the hidden passage, the final showdown with the cookie-loving culprit.

But amidst the celebratory chatter, a moment of realization dawned on Maya. "Wow," she exclaimed, taking a bite of her delicious creation. "We used so much math to solve this case, and we didn't even realize it!"

Ben's eyes lit up in agreement. "You're right! Deciphering coordinates, calculating measurements, analyzing data – all those skills helped us crack the code and save the cookies!"

Charlie, ever the enthusiastic baker, chimed in, "And don't forget about ratios in the dough, percentages for perfect sweetness, and even a sprinkle of decimals for precise baking times!"

As they reminisced, they each highlighted the different math concepts that played a crucial role in their success:

- **Geometry** helped them decipher the coordinates leading to the hidden entrance.
- **Measurement** skills were essential for navigating the secret passage based on coded dimensions.
- **Data analysis** allowed them to interpret the charts and graphs in the villain's lair, revealing clues about their activities.
- **Probability and statistics** empowered them to calculate the chances of finding the culprit in each location.

- **Basic mathematical operations** like percentages, ratios, and decimals proved invaluable during baking and even while disarming the cookie catapult.

Looking back, they realized that math wasn't just about numbers in a textbook. It was a powerful tool that could be applied to solve real-world problems, from cracking codes to achieving baking perfection.

Celebrating Math Skills:

Here are some activities you can do with your readers to celebrate the importance of math in this story:

- **Math Scavenger Hunt:** Create a scavenger hunt around the house or classroom, hiding clues that require basic math skills like addition, subtraction, multiplication, and division to find.
- **Code-Cracking Challenge:** Design a simple code using symbols or numbers and have your readers decipher it using the concepts from the story (e.g., a symbol representing addition, another for multiplication).
- **Real-World Math Challenge:** Present real-world scenarios where math skills are used in everyday life, like calculating recipe ingredients, estimating grocery bills, or measuring for furniture placement.

By engaging in these activities, readers can reinforce the connection between math concepts and their practical applications in various situations.

Chapter 25: The Next Challenge

A Message for the Future!

◈ **Plot:** They receive a coded message hinting at a future adventure, planting the seeds for a sequel.

◈ **Defining Number:** Teaser for future math challenges

◈ **Activities:** Discuss the potential new math challenges they might face in the future, brainstorm ways to use math to solve them.

◈ **Tips & Tricks:** Leave the reader excited about using math skills for future adventures.

Victorious and basking in the warm glow of their achievement, Maya, Ben, and Charlie reveled in the sweet success of their first adventure. They had not only saved the cookies from the clutches of a cunning villain but also discovered the power of teamwork and the magic of math.

As they were packing up the last of their celebratory cookies, a glint of light caught Maya's eye. Tucked beneath an empty plate lay a small, folded piece of paper. Curiosity piqued, she carefully unfolded it.

The paper wasn't blank. Inscribed upon it was a series of cryptic symbols, unlike any they had encountered before. It wasn't a code they recognized – numbers were interwoven with strange shapes and swirling patterns.

"What is this?"

Ben asked, peering over Maya's shoulder, his voice laced with intrigue.

Charlie, ever the optimist, grinned. "Looks like another message for our favorite junior detectives," they declared, a playful glint in their eyes.

"But this code is completely different," Maya pointed out, a frown creasing her forehead. "We don't even know where to begin!"

Undeterred, Ben snatched a napkin and scribbled down some notes. "Maybe it's a new kind of code," he mused, tapping his chin thoughtfully. "A cipher perhaps, or even some kind of geometric code!"

A spark of excitement ignited in Maya's eyes. The thrill of the unknown, the challenge of a new code – it was like a siren song, beckoning them towards another adventure.

"Well, then," Maya declared, a determined glint in her voice, "I guess it's time to brush up on our code-breaking skills and explore this new math mystery. Who's in?"

Charlie and Ben exchanged a look, a silent understanding passing between them. With a chorus of enthusiastic replies, the trio knew one thing for sure – their journey with math, cookies, and exciting adventures was far from over. The message, though cryptic, held the promise of a new challenge, a chance to delve deeper into the fascinating world of numbers and codes.

Activities:

- **Brainstorming Future Challenges:** Have your readers brainstorm what kind of math challenges Maya, Ben, and Charlie might face in their next adventure. Could it involve a new type of code, like a geometric code or a cipher, as hinted at in the story?
- **Math Preparation:** Encourage readers to research different coding methods and explore various mathematical concepts that might be helpful in solving future mysteries.
- **Reader-Created Challenges:** Challenge your readers to create their own math mysteries for Maya, Ben, and Charlie to solve. What kind of code would they use? What math skills would be needed to crack it?

By engaging in these activities, readers can generate excitement about using math skills to tackle future challenges and embark on their own mathematical adventures!

Don't miss out!

Visit the website below and you can sign up to receive emails whenever Rekha Kumari publishes a new book. There's no charge and no obligation.

https://books2read.com/r/B-A-QAJFB-DQYBD

BOOKS 2 READ

Connecting independent readers to independent writers.

Did you love *Operation Awesome: Cracking the Code with Math*? Then you should read *BODMAS Blast Off: A Fun Way to Master Maths*[1] by Rekha Kumari!

[2]

Blast Off into Math Mastery with BODMAS Blast Off

Is your child struggling with order of operations?

BODMAS Blast Off: A Fun Way to Master Maths is the perfect solution!

This exciting book transforms learning BODMAS (Brackets, Of [Multiplication and Division], Multiplication and Division [left to right], Addition and Subtraction [left to right]) into an intergalactic adventure! Join Captain Bracket, Officer Of, Sergeant Times, and the rest of the BODMAS crew as they embark on thrilling missions that require them to use their BODMAS skills to save the day.

---

1. https://books2read.com/u/mBnPYN

2. https://books2read.com/u/mBnPYN

Here's what makes BODMAS Blast Off! a must-read:

Engaging Story: Follow the BODMAS crew through captivating stories filled with spaceships, robots, aliens, and exciting challenges.**Learning Through Play:** Each chapter features a fun and interactive activity that reinforces the BODMAS rule being introduced. Activities include board games, puzzles, coloring sheets, and creative projects.**Multiple Learning Levels:** The book progresses from basic BODMAS concepts to more complex challenges, catering to a range of learning abilities.**Real-World Applications:** Children will discover how BODMAS is used in everyday situations, from shopping and cooking to planning parties and building treehouses.**Fun & Colorful Illustrations:** Vivid and engaging illustrations bring the stories and characters to life, making learning enjoyable.**Builds Confidence:** By successfully completing activities and solving problems, children will gain confidence in their BODMAS skills.**Perfect for All Learners:** This book caters to both visual and kinesthetic learners, with a variety of activities that appeal to different learning styles.**Sets the Stage for Future Math Success:** A strong foundation in BODMAS is essential for mastering more complex math concepts in the future.

More than just a math book, BODMAS Blast Off is an exciting adventure that will transform your child's learning experience. So, buckle up and get ready to blast off into a world of fun and mathematical mastery!

Also by Rekha Kumari

About the Author

Rekha Kumari is a dynamic and accomplished individual, embodying the roles of both an expert entrepreneur and a passionate educator. With a wealth of experience in both fields, she has dedicated her life to empowering children and guiding them towards success.

As a seasoned entrepreneur, Rekha has navigated the complexities of the business world with finesse. Her innovative ideas, strategic vision, and unwavering determination have enabled her to establish herself as a leader in her industry. Through her ventures, she has not only achieved significant professional milestones but has also served as an inspiration to aspiring entrepreneurs, especially women, encouraging them to pursue their dreams fearlessly.

In addition to her entrepreneurial endeavors, Rekha is deeply committed to education and believes in the transformative power it holds. As a teacher, she goes beyond imparting knowledge; she nurtures young minds, instilling in them the values of resilience, determination, and excellence. Her teaching philosophy revolves around building strong foundations and fostering a growth mindset, equipping her students with the tools they need to become winners in life.

Rekha Kumari's unique blend of entrepreneurial acumen and educational expertise makes her a sought-after figure in both business and academic circles. Her dedication to empowering the next generation underscores her belief in the limitless potential of every child. Through her guidance and mentorship, she continues to shape future leaders and pave the way for a brighter tomorrow.

www.ingramcontent.com/pod-product-compliance
Lightning Source LLC
Chambersburg PA
CBHW022146150726
47992CB00002B/775